Religion: A Gateway to Bondage

Religion

A Gateway to Bondage

Robert Johnson

Printed in the United States of America
Copyright © 2023 Robert Johnson

ISBN: 979-8-218-23416-4
Publisher: Robert Johnson

All rights reserved solely by the author. No part of this book may be reproduced, scanned, or distributed in any printed or electronic form without permission.

Scriptures marked KJV are taken from the King James Version, public domain.

Scripture taken from the New King James Version®. Copyright © 1982 by Thomas Nelson. Used by permission. All rights reserved.

Scripture quotations taken from the Amplified® Bible (AMPC), Copyright © 1954, 1958, 1962, 1964, 1965, 1987 by The Lockman Foundation. Used by permission. lockman.org

Table of Contents

Dedication..................................Pg 6

Acknowledgements....................Pg 7

Introduction...............................Pg 9

Chapter 1: How It All Started............Pg 17

Chapter 2: Who's Your Daddy; Not What's Your Religion?......................Pg 23

Chapter 3: Three Part Beings.............Pg 30

Chapter 4: A Crisis of Identity...........Pg 38

Chapter 5: Religion is Outside of God's Love....................................Pg 45

Chapter 6: Right Person in the Wrong Environment........................Pg 52

Chapter 7: It's Not Your Fault!!!..........Pg 63

Chapter 8: The Mind.........................Pg 70

Dedication

To my wife, Nina Lisa Johnson:
I would not have been able to start or complete this task without your prayers and encouragement. Your unselfish attitude and concern allowed me to be confident in what the Lord was saying to me. Although you were going through your life situations, you still were very supportive.
I love you so very much!!

To my daughters: Nina Danielle and Tiffany Nicole
Thank you for taking care of your mother and other things while I was engulfed with the mental challenge of staying focused to complete this work.
You Guys Are the Best. Love Yah!!!

To the Late Great Rev. Dr. Wiley T. Hill Sr.
To my first pastor whom I have had the pleasure and privilege of knowing for over 45 years. This man of God has poured into me the foundational truth of who Jesus really is. Not by Religion, but by the Spirit of God. One of his favorite scriptures was:

"To whom God would make known what is the riches of the glory of this mystery among the Gentiles; which is **CHRIST IN YOU,** the hope of glory." (Colossians 1:27 KJV)

Thank you, Sir, for being obedient to the Spirit of God
Love Yah!!!!

Acknowledgements

First and foremost, we give thanks to our Lord and Savior, Jesus Christ, The Holy Spirit, and my Father God for the opportunity to share what He has given us.

To my Bishop and Pastor, John & Isha Edmondson Thank you for being so transparent in the Spirit. Because of your faithfulness to God's Word, you have propelled me to write this book. May the Lord continue to pour into each of you more Revelational Knowledge.

We Love You Both for Life. God Bless!!!

To my brother and friend: Walter Lewis Sr. Thank you for being there to support the task at hand. Through your persistent encouragement and spiritual insight, I was able to finish this writing. You didn't just do it in words only but also through your actions.

God bless. Love Yah!!!

To my sister: Giselle Quintanilla
You have given me more of an understanding of what you really do in the writing industry.
May God continue to bless and keep all that you endeavor to do.
Again, thank you so very much. God Bless. Love Yah!!!

To Kisha and Mark:
Thank you for your vision which displays and relates to my idea in this book. We would not hesitate to use your services again.

Again, thank you. God Bless.

Introduction

My name is Robert LaVel Johnson. The book you are about to read, Religion: A Gateway to Bondage, is a mandate that the Lord has laid on my heart to inform His people of the dangers of being side-tracked by religion. There are those who have been in the church for many years not knowing the difference between religion and life, and therefore have taught others solely on religion. We have been taught to believe in a religion and following religion instead of believing in a way of life and living. However, when you are taught rightly, you will believe rightly, and when you believe right, you will live right. The sole purpose of this book is to help you understand the difference between religion and life, to embrace living free from bondage. In the following scriptures, you'll see the evidence for being taught right, believing right, and living right.

Being Taught Right: God only dealt with two individuals concerning sin. The two individuals were Adam and Jesus, not religion.

12) Therefore, as sin came into the world by one man, and death as the result of sin, so death spread to all men. [no one being able to stop it or to escape its power] because all men sinned.

17) For if because of one man's trespass (lapse, offense) death reigned through that one, much more surely will those who receive [God's] overflowing grace (unmerited favor) and the free gift of righteousness [putting them into right standing with Himself] reign as kings in life through the one Man Jesus Christ (the Messiah, the Anointed One).

18) Well then, as one man's trespass [one man's false step and falling away led] to condemnation for all men, so one Man's act of righteousness [leads] to acquittal and right standing with God and life for all men.

19) For just as by one man's disobedience (failing to hear, heedlessness, and carelessness) the many were constituted sinners, so by one Man's obedience many will be constituted righteous (made acceptable to God, brought into right standing with Him).

Romans 5:12, 17-19 (AMPC)

Believing Right:

8) But what does it say? The Word (God's message in Christ) is near you, on your lips and in your heart; that is, the Word (the message, the basis and object) of faith which we preach,

9) Because if you acknowledge and confess with your lips that Jesus is Lord and in your heart believe (adhere to, trust in, and rely on the truth) that God raised Him from the dead, you will be saved.

10) For with the heart a person believes (adheres to, trusts in, and relies on Christ) and so is justified (declared righteous, acceptable to

God), and with the mouth he confesses (declares openly and speaks out freely his faith) and confirms [his] salvation.

Romans 10:8-10 (AMPC)

Living Right:

20) I am crucified with Christ [in Him I have shared His crucifixion] it is no longer I who live, but Christ (the Messiah) lives in me; and the life I now live in the body I live by the faith in (by adherence to and reliance on and complete trust in) the Son of God, who loved me and gave Himself up for me. Galatians 2:20 (AMPC)

8) For it is by free grace (God's unmerited favor) that you are saved (delivered from judgement and made partakers of Christ's salvation) through [your] faith. And this [salvation] is not of yourselves [of your own doing, it came not through your own striving], but it is the gift of God.

9) Not because of your works [not the fulfillment of the Law's demands], lest any man should boast. [it is not the results of what anyone could possibly do, so no one can pride himself in it or take glory for himself.]

10) For we are God's [own] handiwork (His workmanship), recreated in Christ Jesus, [born anew) that we may do those good works which God had predestinated (planned beforehand) for us [taking path which he prepared ahead of time], that we should walk in them [living the good life which he prearranged and made ready for us to live].

Ephesians 2:8-10 (AMPC)

However, we were never taught that we are spirit beings having a temporary human experience on the earth. This book is to remind everyone that Jesus never spoke of a religion, He was always concerned about life and our need to have a change of life experience, not a change of religion. Getting to know who you really are and why you are here on earth.

While writing this book, our world is in an epidemic namely the Coronavirus which began on March 13th in the year 2020. We have been bombarded with 2.667,528 deaths and 120 million have been affected by the virus worldwide within a year. (Wikipedia)

The church organizations have closed, the non-essential agencies and stores have been ordered to close as well. In the United States, the state of New York is the epicenter of this situation. Everyone has been ordered to wear a mask, and if we are to go outside, we must make sure to stay at least 6 feet apart from each other. We are banned from the parks, playgrounds, gyms, and other physically and densely populated sites.

The Presidential voting machine has been halted. Every normal and daily routine has changed. Millions of people have lost their jobs. All of the schools have been closed, and the sports world has been cancelled and ceased to entertain indefinitely. I pray that this book will inform you, the reader, that religion had nothing to do with the recovery of this epidemic. It was the love, mercy, and grace of God.

This is the deadliest health epidemic in the history of the United States since the Spanish Flu in 1918 over 100 years ago. The Spanish Flu was reported to have originated in China which took 5 million lives and infected over 500 million individuals.

There is nothing religious about what we are going through. Typically in times as these, we have always needed someone or something to deliver or correct or heal our nation. The Coronavirus is not exclusive to a certain religion; it does not consider religion, race, or social class. There must be a stronger and much mightier law that supersedes this pandemic, Not Religion.

This is why Jesus came to earth to knock down the walls of religion and establish His love and grace and mercy towards the world. Not Religion. This is why I am writing this book. Every day there are people trapped in the bondage of religion without the understanding that religion cannot save lives. The pandemic was proof of that. So, it is my mission to free others from the gateway of bondage, once and for all.

"For God did not send His Son into the world to condemn the world, but that the world through Him might be saved." John 3:17 (NKJV)

Chapter 1
How It All Started

Chapter 1
How It All Started

If you take a close look at the origin of time, it stipulates in Genesis 1:1 and John 1:1 that, "In The Beginning GOD...", it does not say in the beginning religion. If you look at the world today, you will find that about 84% of the world's population believe in a religion. Let's understand that religion has played a major part in division and separation while trying to control the everyday functions of your life. What do we say when we speak or mention the word *religion*? How is it interpreted in your life? Let's find out the true meaning or definition of the word religion and where it came from.

The word *Religion* comes from the root word in the Latin verb ligo, comes religion, to tie or bind over again.

Religo comes from the substantive religio, which, with the addition of the letter n makes the English substantive religion.

RELIGION: (its origin) Latin- religare, To re-bind.

The Latin word religio means Obligation, Bond, Happy, Reverence

In OLD FRENCH Religion is Life under monastic Vows

(Peter Hulen – Religion – Personal Web Page – Wabash College)

From the definitions and origins, we know that religion at its root is purposed to bind or tie. And when something is bound, it cannot move. As we see, the impression that we were given to be religious has been a detriment to our spiritual growth. It has pressured us to try to be more Christ like according to what we think is right, when in fact it has hindered who we really should be or become or who we really are in Christ.

There are 4300 religions in the world today, (This is according to Adherents, an independent, non-religiously affiliated organization that monitors the number and size of the worlds religions) which causes one to wonder, which is or who has the correct religion. As you read further, you will find that religion really is a gateway to bondage.

Just to name a few of the most popular religions:

Christianity - 2.22 billion followers

Islam - 1.65 billion followers

Hinduism - 1.05 billion followers

Buddhism - 488 million followers

These are your major religions in the world, which we worship. Each religion has its means of worship, beliefs, or conduct which feeds into a subservient (prepared to obey unquestioningly) atmosphere. We were told for many years that we were to do or work in order to get God's approval and acceptance. However, why would you work for something that has already been paid for or has already been purchased for you? God's approval and acceptance is a gift.

For it is by free grace (God's unmerited favor) that ye are saved (delivered from judgement and made partakers of Christ's salvation) through [your] faith. And this [salvation] is not of yourselves [of your own doing, it came not through your own striving], but it is the gift of God: Not because of works [not the fulfillment of the Law's demands], lest any man should boast. [it is not the results of what anyone can possibly do, so no one can pride himself in it or take glory to himself.] Ephesians 2:8-9 (AMPC)

For example, just imagine you've gone to the supermarket to buy a loaf of bread. You get to the register and the total amount due is $2.50. You then use whatever manner of payment to purchase the loaf of bread. You grab the loaf of bread and walk out of the supermarket to go home. Then the next day, you return to the same supermarket with that same loaf of bread with the intent to pay for it even though it was already paid for. Remember, the bread was paid for yesterday, so why are you paying again for something that has already been purchased? The price was paid!!!!!!

18) Forasmuch as ye know that ye were not redeemed with corruptible things, as silver and gold, from your vain conversation received by tradition from your fathers;

19) But with the precious blood of Christ, as of a lamb without blemish and without spot.

1 Peter 1:18-19 (KJV)

20) For ye are bought with a price: therefore, glorify God in your body, and in your spirit, which are God's.

1 Corinthians 6:20 (KJV)

God's acceptance and approval of you is already for you. His grace and redemption has nothing to do with religion. Religion started in a way that made everyone believe they needed to do more of something. But there's nothing you need to continue to do or anything more you can do to gain God's approval.

Chapter 2:

Who's Your Daddy; Not What's Your Religion?

Chapter 2:

Who's Your Daddy; Not What's Your Religion?

When Jesus was on the earth, He never spoke about religion. He always spoke about who His Father was and where He came from, and Jesus was our example on the earth of how we should live. Jesus did not come to earth to start a religion, but to put an end to religions that bind you into a forced way of life. Jesus came to make us free.

31) Then said Jesus to those Jews which believed on him, if ye continue in my word, then are ye my disciples indeed; 32) And ye shall know the truth, and the truth shall make you free. John 8:31-32 (KJV).

God never planned for man to be religious, but to have life and that more abundantly. To live freely in Christ Jesus.

The thief comes only but for to steal, and to kill, and to destroy. I came that they might have and enjoy life and have it in abundance (to the full till it overflows).

John 10:10 (AMPC)

Let's start with the very first book in the Bible which is Genesis.

Genesis 1:1 reads,

> 1) In the beginning God created the heaven and the earth.

There is no information in this scripture that states that in the beginning religion created the heavens and the earth. In fact, there is nothing that says religion at all. If we continue to read, in the 26th verse of the same chapter it says,

26) And God said, Let us make man in our image, according to our likeness: and let them have dominion over the fish of the sea, and over the fowl of the air, and over the cattle, and over all the earth, and over every creeping thing that creepeth upon the earth.

So God created man in His own image, we were made in the image and likeness of The Father (God), The Son or the Word (Jesus), and the Holy Ghost (Comforter), which they are One Spirit. I don't care who you are or where you come from, you are made in the image and likeness of God.

This is the beginning of mankind from God Himself.

You will see that from the first day of creation, through the sixth day, it stipulates that God created everything that exists as it says in John 1:1-3

> 1) In the beginning was the Word, and the Word was with God, and the Word was God.
> 2) The same was in the beginning with God.
> 3) All things were made by Him, and without Him was not anything made that was made.

When it speaks of seed after its own kind in Genesis 1:11-25, it never mentioned that the seed had to be subjected to brain washing or taught what to do under manmade regulations. The seed automatically has in it all that it needs to be the seed that it was made to be. If you plant a delicious red apple seed in the ground, you can't expect to get a sour green apple at harvest. The seed that's planted is the seed that will produce after its own kind. The seed in the natural that mostly describes the scripture, after its own kind is the acorn.

The acorn is a nut of the oak tree. Everything that the acorn needs to become a 33 to 131 ft. oak tree is on the inside of it. You will never get a cherry tree or an apple tree from an acorn, but you will get an oak tree from an acorn. Even though the acorn is small and hard shelled what it needs to produce after its own kind is already on the inside of it.

In Genesis 1:26, God said, "Let us make man in our image and after our likeness...." The phrase, "after its own kind" is mentioned 10 times in the first chapter of Genesis in the Bible. There is a major reason why God started everything off with the phrase, "after its own kind".

On the 3rd day God – after its own kind

On the 5th day God – after its own kind

On the 6th day God – after its own kind

All our lives are to be governed by the life that's on the inside of us. Not governed by religion nor "dos and don'ts" but by the power or life that is on the inside of us.

1) Being born again, not of corruptible seed, but of incorruptible, by the word of God,

which liveth and abideth forever." 1Peter 1:23 (KJV)

When God made us, He created us in His direct image and after His likeness. When Adam and Eve were beguiled by the serpent, there was a change in the planting process. So, everyone who is born after that event and (after what took place at Calvary) who has not received Jesus as their personal Savior, now has a different seed in them. If Adam and Eve really knew who they were, they would have told Satan to shut up and go sit down the very second he began to talk.

Now that we have a different seed in us, we lean to and learn from the seed and its control that is in us or the seed, after its own kind. This is the main reason why there is a need to be born again. This process will change the seed we have, to the seed which we were to become from the beginning.

Just as the animals live after their own kind, so do we as human beings. The main focus here is that we aren't human beings, we are spirit beings. This is what our seed was from the beginning and still is. So, when we become born again, we go back to the seed that was from the beginning. The seed that was in His image and after His likeness.

24) God is a Spirit, (a spiritual being) and those who worship Him must worship Him in spirit and truth (reality).

John 4:24 (AMPC)

His (God's) image and likeness is Spirit. This is who we really are.

As we grow in our new birth, the seed will begin to mature after its own kind. The problem will not be the seed of our new birth, but the mental seed or programming which occurred when we were taught to believe what the old seed was producing.

The seed you water will grow. If we continue to water the mental seed of our lives, then the religious thought patterns will continue to grow. But, if we continue to water our spiritual seed, (the one created in God's image), then the supernatural revelational knowledge of Jesus will continue to grow up in us after its own kind. Let's water the right seed.

Chapter 3:
Three Part Beings

Chapter 3:
Three Part Beings

The next thing God performed, after the creation of heaven and earth, was the creation of man from the dust of the ground.

7) And the Lord God formed man of the dust of the ground and breathed into his nostrils the breath of life; and man became a living soul. Genesis 2:7 (KJV),

Now, here we have the three parts of man:

Spirit, Soul, and Body.

The part that comes directly from God was and is the Spirit, then God breathed into man the breath of life and man became a living soul.

In man dwells the main part of the tri-union, which is the spirit, which was created for God himself to live. Then you have the part which is called the Soul or the mind, which controls our will, emotions, and our intellect. Lastly, you have the body which houses the Spirit and the Soul. Let's explore the definition of each part of man for better understanding.

We are a spirit:

Spirit: The Greek word for Spirit is pneuma which has a similar meaning to the word ruach. Pneuma means to breathe or blow, and primarily denotes the wind. Breath: the spirit which, like the wind, is invisible, immaterial, and powerful. Your spirit is the dwelling place for the Spirit of God.

We possess a soul:

Soul/Mind: The element of a person that enables them to be aware of the world and their experiences; to think or feel, the faculty consciousness and thought. Example: As the thought ran through his mind, he came to a conclusion.

We live in a body:

Body: temples or houses your soul and spirit. It is the part of you needed to operate on earth. "What? know ye not that your body is the temple of the Holy Ghost, which is in you, which ye have of God, and ye are not your own?" 1 Corinthians 6:19 (KJV)

Let's take a look at why it was so important that Jesus became our sacrifice.

Remember that God is a God of order. So, when sin entered into the world, there had to be a legal change to correct the fall of man. It was a man (Adam) that started this sinful nature we are born with so, it had to be a Man (Jesus) to undo and correct the whole situation. See the scriptures below for reference.

12) Therefore, as sin came into the world through one man, and death as the result of sin, so death spread to all men [no one being able to stop it or to escape its power], because all men sinned.

13) [To be sure] sin was in the world before ever the Law was given, but sin is not charged to men's account when there is no law [to transgress].

14) Yet death held sway from Adam to Moses [the Lawgiver], even over those who did not themselves transgress [a positive command] as Adam did. Adam was a type (prefigure) of the One Who was to come [in reverse, the former destructive, the Latter saving].

15) But God's free gift is not at all to be compared to the trespass [His grace is out of all

proportion to the fall of man]. For if many died through one man's falling away (his lapse, his offense), much more profusely did God's grace and the free gift [that comes] through the undeserved favor of the one Man Jesus Christ abound *and* overflow to *and* for [the benefit of] many.

16) Nor is the free gift at all to be compared to the effect of that one [man's] sin. For the sentence [following the trespass] of one [man] brought condemnation, whereas the free gift [following] many transgressions brings justification (an act of righteousness).

17) For if because of one man's trespass (lapse, offense) death reigned through that one, much more surely will those who receive [God's] overflowing grace (unmerited favor) and the free gift of righteousness [putting them into right standing with Himself] reign as kings in life through the one man Jesus Christ (the Messiah, the Anointed One).

18) Well then, as one man's trespass [one man's false step and falling away led] to condemnation for all men, so one Man's act of righteousness [leads] to acquittal *and* right standing with God and life for all men.

19) For just as by one man's disobedience (failing to hear, heedlessness, and carelessness) the many were constituted sinners, so by one Man's obedience the many will be constituted righteous (made acceptable to God, brought into right standing with Him).

Romans 5:12-19 (AMPC)

So, Jesus had to become what we were in order for us to become who He is.

17) Therefore if any person is [ingrafted] in Christ (the Messiah) he is a new creation (a new creature altogether); the old [previous moral and spiritual condition] has passed away. Behold, the fresh *and* new has come!

18) But all things are from God, Who through *Jesus* Christ reconciled us to Himself [received us into favor, brought us into harmony with Himself] and gave to us the ministry of reconciliation [that by word and deed we might aim to bring others into harmony with Him].

19) It was God [personally present] in Christ, reconciling *and* restoring the world to favor with Himself, not counting up *and* holding against [men] their trespasses but cancelling them], and

committing unto us the message of reconciliation (of the restoration to favor).

20) So we are Christ's ambassadors, God making His appeal as it were through us. We [as Christ's personal representatives] beg you for His sake to lay hold of the divine favor [now offered you] *and* be reconciled to God.

21) For our sake He made Christ to be sin, Who knew no sin, so that in *and* through Him we might become [endued with, viewed as being in, and examples of] the righteousness of God [what we ought to be, approved and acceptable and in right relationship with Him, by His goodness].

2 Corinthians 5:17-21 (AMPC)

All of this was done in the Spirit part of Man, the real you. So, where did religion come into play and what is pure religion? Pure religion, undefined before God and the Father is this: to visit the fatherless and widows in their affliction, and to keep himself unspotted from the world. (James 1:27 AMPC)

Religion has made it so that even the place of worship has become a place of do's and don'ts instead of a place of thanks and worship for what Jesus has already done for us. The place where we should be able to come for anything that pertains to meeting our needs in Life, Love, and Peace, has become a place of downtrodden children of God who really don't know who they are.

Now that you have become a new creation in Christ Jesus the past has passed, even though religion has made us guilty of all our past, making us responsible for caring and carrying the pain of the past and responsible for getting rid of it. Why? When Jesus has already paid the cost of my past, present, and future sins.

"As far as the east is from the west, so far has he removed our transgressions from us."
Psalm 103:12 (AMPC)

"For I will be gracious and merciful towards their sins, and I will remember their deeds of unrighteousness no more."
Hebrews 8:12 (AMPC)

"So, brethren, we [who are born again] are not children of a slave woman [the natural], but of the free [the supernatural]."
Galatians 4:31 (AMPC)

Chapter 4:
A Crisis of Identity

Chapter 4:
A Crisis of Identity

Religion comes from the fleshy realm, based on human ingenuity. God's life is based on the Supernatural realm which comes from the Spiritual Promise realm. Religion is a mental ascent function, while God's life is based on and comes from a revelational knowledge. Religion has nothing to do with the Spirit of God.

Religion has become a rope that has been applied around the neck of your mind. As an elephant cannot get rid of that binding rope no matter how much older or how much larger it gets, it still has a fear of breaking loose to be who they really are because they have been conditioned.

There is an identity in the animal kingdom in which each animal plays a part. There are some who live in trees, there are some who live in burrows in the ground, and there are some who live on the plains or flat lands. These are animals that can become the most vicious and deadliest creatures on earth because they know who they are. But there are those animals who have been trapped in the mind game. Let me explain. Have you ever been to a circus where there are Lions, Tigers...and Bears (oh my)? Every animal in the big tent has been inducted into the Hall of Shame named, "If You Only Knew"!!!

These animals are ferocious. But each animal has to be mentally brainwashed to become who they are NOT. They have to be subjected to the many changes of thought patterns that control the actions of their everyday life.

Take for example, the mighty elephant. When an elephant is a baby in the circus, the way it is controlled is by a chain which is tied around its leg and a stake that is hammered into the ground which doesn't allow the elephant to pull it out. As the years go by, the elephant has grown to an enormously large size and has the physical strength to tear apart anything in its path. It has the strength to break free. But it does not know that because it still has the mental thought pattern of not being able to get away from the chain that has the elephant under its control.

Proverbs 23:7. If you only knew!!!

In the wild or in the world of freedom where all the animals' lives began, they were not subjected to having to think of what to do or how to do it.

When it came time for food, they knew exactly what to do. When it was time to provide shelter, they knew exactly what to do. When it was time to protect, they knew exactly what to do. They never needed to be taught how to eat, fight, or provide shelter. These things came naturally to them. Why? Because they were living out of their identity or who they were created to be. What is Identity?

Identity: The fact of being who or what a person or thing is.

Religion even causes you to perform the rituals of touch not, taste not, handle not after the commandments and doctrines of men. Indeed such practices have the outward appearance (that popularly passes) for wisdom, in promoting self-imposed rigor of devotion and delight in self-humiliation and severity of discipline of the body, but they are of no value in checking the indulgence of the flesh (the lower nature). Instead, they do not honor God but serve only to indulge the flesh. (Col. 2:20-23)

"Not by might, nor by power but by my spirit saith the Lord." (Zechariah. 4:6)

As it also states in Isaiah 55:9, "For as the heavens are higher than the earth, so are my ways higher than your ways and my thoughts than your thoughts." We celebrate a time in the Christian religion which is called Easter (or Resurrection Sunday), which is the crucifixion, death, burial and resurrection of our Lord and Savior Jesus Christ. Let's unpack this for a minute.

Crucifixion - the execution of a person by nailing or binding them to a cross. Greek definition: Raising up, or rising up, from the Greek word Anastasia.

Burial - the action or practice of interning a dead body.

Death - the end of the life of a person or organism

Resurrection - the action or fact of resurrecting or being resurrected.

None of this (the crucifixion, death, and burial of Christ) nor the day in which it's celebrated has anything to do with religion. It has nothing to do with a "do or don't" philosophy. It has nothing to do with a dress code. There is not a religion that can save a person from their sins. It had to be a person. This is why it's stated in Matthew 1:21, *he shall save his people from their sins.*

But the religious could not fathom something so "simple". Even Jesus was ridiculed for healing a man on the Sabbath day. If you read, John 5:15-16, you will find that the Jews were more concerned about what the law (religion) said instead of being concerned on what the law giver (of grace) was saying. Isn't it strange that we have more faith in what we are doing, instead of what He has already done for us?

Growing up in the church from a young age, we were taught that we were a set of people called Pentecostals or Holy Rollers. If we saw someone that didn't act like us or talk like us, we would think of them as being wrong and sinful. We would tell those who did not act like us that they were on their way to hell if they didn't get right with God. This caused a separation in communication because we felt we were better than they were and that they really needed to get Jesus the "right way". What caused us to think that way? Religion causes us to become prideful which the Word of God says is an abomination to God in Proverbs 6:16-19.

Religion causes discrimination and causes people to look at each other in a judgmental way. It causes you to think that you are a better individual than others because you see them doing something that you don't think they should be doing. We forget that the Word of God says in Romans 3:23 (KJV),

"For ALL have sinned and come short of the glory of God."

This didn't happen when you committed the act of sin, it happened in the garden of Eden from the beginning of man.

You don't have to sin to become a sinner, all you need to do is be born. As soon as we are born, we're born into sin because of what happened in the garden. Yet, this is how religion has put destructive thoughts in our minds to think that we are the problem instead of putting in our minds that Jesus is the answer to the problems in our lives.

Chapter 5:
Religion is Outside of God's Love

Chapter 5:
Religion is Outside of God's Love

God has made us human beings not human doings. We are to be who we are. Who are we?????

We are spirit beings having a temporary human experience.

For in him we live, we move, and we have our being as stated in Acts 17:28. For the life that we now live in the flesh we live it by the faith of the Son of God who loved us and gave himself for us. Knowing this, that nothing shall be able to separate me from the love of God, which is in Christ Jesus, for it is Christ in me the hope of glory.

I don't accept who I am by how I feel, I accept who I am by knowing that it is already finished; that is, the work of Christ who lives in me. This is my identity. And in God's love there is no place for religion.

Think about this, while waiting for a certain check to arrive, with anticipation, excitement sets in. Knowing that, if not today, the check would still be coming to us. The feeling of security that, if the check doesn't come today, it has already been sent and is waiting for me to pick it up. The Lord wants us to be that excited and wait in anticipation even if we don't see it with our physical eyes or any of our five senses. He wants us to know that it's already DONE!!! (IT IS FINISHED !!!) just receive it!!

Why do we try to work a work that has already been worked?

Religion will assure you that if you do or perform this, then he will do that. What we fail to see is that he has already done that which we are working so hard to complete and accomplish, not knowing that all it requires is that we believe and accept what is already finished.

If we continue to work for something that has already been taken care of, then it's not faith, it's wishing.

"Jesus said to him, because you have seen Me, *Thomas,* do you now believe (trust and have faith)? Blessed *and* happy *and* to be envied *are* those who have never seen Me and *yet* have believed *and* adhered to *and* trusted *and* relied on Me." John 20:29 (AMPC)

Faith sees a finished work, not on the basis of what you do but on the foundation of what Jesus did on Calvary. Jesus spoke very clearly concerning religion in his day. He spoke a scripture that deals with this directly.

In the book of Matthew the eleventh chapter, John the Baptist, while in prison, heard of the miracles and works which Jesus had performed. He sent two of his disciples to see if He (Jesus) was the real deal, or do I have to look for another? Jesus responded to John (in verse 5) by saying, "The blind receive their sight, the lame walk, the lepers are cleansed, and the deaf hear, the dead are raised up, and the poor have the gospel preached to them." The more Jesus speaks in the chapter, the more you will find that there were fractions of Jews that were looking for Jesus to come looking and acting a certain way.

Jesus was informing them (the Jews) that he knew what they were saying and thinking. This is a religious thought pattern even amongst God's people today.

"The Son of man came eating and drinking, and they say, Behold a man gluttonous, and a winebibber, a friend of publicans and sinners...." (Matthew 11:19)

Jesus had to call out to those who really believed in who He was. In verses 28-30 of the same chapter, Jesus called out to all those who were tired of the religious thought patterns and mind games which brings about pride and bondage – not love.

Jesus said, "Come unto me, all ye that labor and are heavy laden *and* overburdened, I will give you rest. [I will ease and refresh your souls.] Take my yoke upon you and learn of me; for I am gentle (meek) and humble (lowly) in heart, and you will find rest (relief and ease and refreshment and recreation and blessed quiet) for your souls.

For my yoke is wholesome (useful, good-not harsh, hard sharp, or pressing, but comfortable, gracious, and pleasant), and My burden is light *and* easy to be borne."
Matthew 11:28-30 (AMPC)

Let me give you a personal experience of how a mind game works on anyone whether it be religious or just an everyday mental situation. I have a cat which was given to us as a pet and also for pest control. He was about 6 weeks old when we received him. As all animals have to adapt to their environment, there also has to be some sort of control. My cat (T.J.) was taught not to climb on furniture or tables or any other place where we sit or eat. The way he is controlled is with a newspaper or anything that sounds like a plastic paper bag. This has been instilled in him since he was a kitten. Long before he had sharp teeth or paws with sharp claws or even the strength and size to pull away. Now 4 years later, he's gained weight and his claws are very sharp and need to be trimmed often, and he has very sharp teeth which can pierce anything that comes in contact with his mouth. With all that physical growth, he still has the same mentality that he had when he was a kitten. Why? Because it's what he has known since he was little.

"Do not be conformed to this world (this age), [fashioned after and adapted to its external, superficial customs], but be transformed (changed) by the [entire] renewal of your mind [by its new ideals and its new attitudes], so that you may prove [for yourselves] what is the good and acceptable and perfect will of God, *even* the thing which is good and acceptable and perfect [in His sight for you]." Romans 12:2 (AMPC)

Although, he is now able to claw and chew his way through anything including me, all I have to do is let him hear the sound of a newspaper or plastic bag and he is gone. Not knowing that he really does not have to listen to me anymore, but he is afraid to break free from the thing that has had him trapped and bound from when he was a kitten. He has been conditioned. This is the same trick Satan does with God's people. He continues to use religion which tells you that you are a sinner saved by grace when (after salvation) you are no longer a sinner you are a born-again child of God. He continues through religion to use the guilt syndrome of dos and don'ts instead of the truth of what Jesus has done.

"Therefore, [there is] now no condemnation (no adjudging guilty of wrong) for those who are in Christ Jesus, *who live [and] walk not after the dictates of the flesh, but after the dictates of the Spirit.*"
Romans 8:1-2 (AMPC)

"Therefore if any person is [ingrafted] in Christ (the Messiah) he is a new creation (a new creature altogether); the old [previous moral and spiritual condition] has passed away. Behold, the fresh *and* new has come!"
2 Corinthians 5:17 (AMPC)

Chapter 6:
Right Person in the Wrong Environment

Chapter 6:

Right Person in the Wrong Environment

The control and guilt of religion will also cause you not to grow in the right place or glow in the right way. Association has a great deal to do with the growth of a believer.

To sanctify means set apart as or declare holy; consecrated.

"Sanctify them through thy truth: thy word is truth," John 17:17 (KJV).

We are set apart through Jesus, Jesus is Truth.

Not through works, lest any man should boast.

IT IS THE GIFT of GOD!! (Ephesians 2:10)

Jesus said, "I am the way, the truth and the life: no man cometh unto the Father but by me," John 14:6b (KJV).

The entire foundation and purpose for religion is to control. In the Old Testament, the three major ways of communication when hearing from God were through the Priest, the King, and the Prophet.

The people would listen to them because that was the only way, at that time, to hear the truth. The Prophet would hear from God then he would tell the King what he heard from God and what was going to happen, then the King would tell the Priest to pray for God's blessings on the people and the land that which he heard from the Prophet.

In those times, direction was always given to the people of the land in that manner. However, the communication situation has been dealt with through the shed blood of Jesus. We now have direct access to the Holy of Holies because of what Jesus completed on Calvary. No longer do we have to hear from three different sources.

"Let us therefore come boldly unto the throne of grace, that we may obtain mercy, and find grace to help in time of need." Hebrews 4:16 (KJV)

Religion also keeps you ignorant of the reality of who you really are. The main reason God's people are destroyed: because they do not know the truth. Hosea 4:6 states that God's people are destroyed for lack of knowledge.

Get to know the true fact of why Jesus was brought here. Jesus was made manifest to destroy the works of the devil (1John 3:8).

This is what Jesus accomplished on Calvary. He (Jesus) destroyed the works of Satan and made a show of him openly in the presence of his imps (Colossians 2: 14-15). Satan and sin has been defeated because of the shed blood of Jesus, not because of anyone's religion.

When we see the whole truth and nothing but the truth, there is very little we have to do to add to this already victorious life. If you study Hebrews 10:1-9, you will see the Word of God specifically say that sacrifice and offerings according to the Law, He takes no pleasure in them. The ritual of the Law is something that He (God the Father) never wanted.

There were 613 commandments given to God's people to keep, when Moses was in conversation with God. His whole purpose and plan was for us to live together as spiritual beings living in His peace and love without sin. He wanted a family of Spirit beings like Him.

I can hear the Spirit of the Lord saying: "Didn't I make you in the image and likeness of us? This is why I had to come down to undo everything that was done which was totally contrary to My will. I will never trust Man with that authority again, that's why I made sure everything was taken care of Myself."

In Hebrews 10:9-14, God is basically saying, "I didn't even want the Tabernacle and priest in the equation, but when man fell there had to be a way to show them that no matter what you try to do to get back to me it can't be done by human ingenuity." The scripture says God used One single sacrifice that was perfect and sanctified all. Not by might, nor by power, but by my Spirit saith the Lord of host. (Zechariah 4:6). Not by works lest any man should boast, it is the gift of God. (Ephesians 2:9).

Let go of every preconceived idea that you have held captive in your mind all these years and let the Spirit of the Lord transform your thinking. The only true thought that we should meditate on is that Jesus is the supreme and only true sacrifice for sin. He has forgiven all of your sins. He became the total sum of sin itself.

"For he hath made him to be sin for us, who knew no sin; that we might be made the righteousness of God in him."
2 Corinthians 5:21 (KJV)

He wiped the slate clean before the sight of God and, by accepting the remedy, has translated you from the kingdom of darkness into the Kingdom of light. Take advantage of what the blood of Jesus has already done which is what you could never do on your own or in any religious act. (Colossians 1:13, 1Peter 2:19)

The Case of Mistaken Identity

There has always been a case of mistaken identity in the church world because of how we were taught. Religion says that we are what we see instead of showing us that we are more what we don't see. Stop associating your behavior with who you really are (your identity). There is a growth pattern on the inside that has to take place in your life on a daily basis in order for you to show on the outside what your true identity really is on the inside.

A prince or princess never wonders whether they will become king or queen when they get older, it's already in their blood or DNA. They become who they really are by growing into it. Their behavior has nothing to do with who they are. The seed in them is royalty so the outcome will be royal.

There is a law which God has implemented in the world before He created Man, which is found in the book of Genesis, and that law is after His kind, or after its kind. Gen. 1:11-12,21,24. (26) Our identity is connected to a source beyond our understanding. 1 Peter 1:4 (Divine Nature)

Identity is the fact of being who or what a person or thing is.

Let's take a glance at the differences between Salvation and Religion:

----Religion is costly,

----Salvation is free.

----Religion will cost you your freedom of life.

----Salvation will give you life, and that more abundantly.

Again, let me restate that religion causes you to become prideful. The Word of God says in Proverbs 16:18 that pride goes before destruction, and a haughty spirit before a fall. When the do's and don'ts become your guideline for being righteous and it controls your judgement towards others, it becomes pride.

This happens when you feel that you don't do what they do and that you are better than they are because you don't do what they do, it's called pride. Christians are the only ones that shoot their wounded walking. But for the Grace of God I would be in the same place. We who are strong are to bear the infirmities of the weak. (Romans 15:1). Remember, you will need a strong brother or sister to bear you up in your weakness, this goes to show that we should never be proud about anything except the Grace of God. Pride causes you to judge others and not look at yourself. This is called *projection*.

Projection is believing that someone else does not like you when it is actually you who does not like them. By projecting this onto another you ascribe the negativity of the thoughts/feelings onto them so that your ego does not have to admit the deficiency of your own thought processes.

No more self-righteousness

Self-righteousness and religion are the same.

Study Romans 4:1-8

The word *justified* means declared righteous. God doesn't get any glory in your righteousness out of what you do. Righteousness comes when you believe God, that makes you righteous, not your works. If you worked for righteousness, then there would be a debt owed but Jesus paid it all.

3) For what does the Scripture say? Abraham believed in (trusted in) God, and it was credited to his account as righteousness (right living and right standing with God).

4) Now to a laborer, his wages are not counted as a favor *or* a gift, but as an obligation (something owed to him).

5) But to one who, not working [by the Law], trusts (believes fully) in Him who justifies the ungodly, his faith is credited to him as righteousness (the standing acceptable to God).

6) Thus David congratulates the man and pronounces a blessing on him to whom God credits righteousness apart from the works he does:

7) Blessed *and* happy *and* to be envied are those whose iniquities are forgiven and whose sins are covered up *and* completely buried.

8) Blessed *and* happy *and* to be envied is the person whose sin the Lord will take no account *nor* reckon it against him.

9) Is this blessing (happiness) then meant only for the circumcised, or also for the uncircumcised? We say that faith was credited to Abraham as righteousness.
Romans 4:3-9 (AMPC)

See also: (Genesis 15:6, Genesis 3:6, James 2:23).

We have to stop praying for God to do something that He has already done. Self-righteousness is trusting in yourself. Religion operates through fear and guilt along with self-righteousness of God's punishment. It will cause you to work on yourself to try to clean up sin. Religion works on what you are doing not on who you are *being*.

The offering of sacrifices has changed and it's no longer your effort to sacrifice but the body of Jesus has become the supreme sacrifice for all.

I am right with God, and all is well. God made Jesus' wisdom, righteousness, sanctification, and redemption (1 Corinthians 1:30).

The very day you accepted Jesus as your personal Savior, this is who you are right now.

"For by a single offering He has forever completely cleansed *and* perfected those who are consecrated and made holy."
Hebrews 10:14 (AMPC)

You are righteous because of Jesus only and nothing else. Not the righteousness of the law, but the righteousness of God by faith. Religion is working on what we are doing, not on what He has done.

"For both he that sanctifieth and they who are sanctified are all of one: for which cause he is not ashamed to call them brethren," (Hebrews 2:11)

When your spiritual garment becomes a costume, then you become a clown. Garment is an item of clothing. A person's mark can be a mark of his or her authority. In the realm of the spirit, everyone is considered to be clothed with one form of garment or the other. Costume: a set of clothes in a style typical of a particular country or historical period. An outfit worn to create the appearance characteristic of a particular period, person, place, or thing.

Chapter 7:
It's Not Your Fault!!!!

Chapter 7:
It's Not Your Fault!!!!

"For all have sinned and fallen short of the glory of God." Romans 3:23 (NKJV)

There is a fear that has captured the minds of the human race that says, "You better get right before you go to hell," or "You are on your way to a devil's place." There is a great amount of fear and discouragement in the world today that makes no one want to know who God the Father really is. Let me try to help erase the fear factor that has caused you to think that God doesn't care, God wouldn't want you, and that being born in sin was your fault.

In the beginning, God made a man and a woman whose names were Adam and Eve. God gave Adam a direct command not to eat from the tree of knowledge of good and evil. There were two trees in the midst of the garden which were the tree of life and the tree of knowledge of good and evil.

8) And the Lord God planted a garden eastward in Eden; and there He put the man whom He had formed.

9) And out of the ground made the Lord God to grow every tree that is pleasant to the sight, and good for food; the tree of life also in the midst of the garden, and the tree of knowledge of good and evil.

Genesis 2:8-9 (KJV)

Here is where it all began!!!!

So, by being disobedient to God sin fell on the entire human race, not just Adam and Eve but on everyone that was born thereafter. In other words, their seed was affected and infected by sin.

16) And the Lord God commanded man, saying, of every tree in the garden thou mayest freely eat:

17) But of the tree of knowledge of good and evil, thou shall not eat of it: for in the day that thou eatest thereof thou shall surely die.

Genesis 2:16-17 (KJV)

Think of it this way, your father and mother is Adam and Eve (so to speak) and your father had a relationship with your mother which produced you, now you are the seed of your parents. So, everything that your parents are, you are. You see the picture? We were in the loins of Adam and Eve and everything that happened to them was passed down to us. That's why all have sinned and fallen short of the glory of God. This is why God is not holding anything to your charge or your fault, you didn't do it. All were born in sin and shaped in iniquity, so stop feeling guilty about that because Jesus came to free you from the guilt of the past and to give you a new future. God only dealt with two people concerning this problem of sin in the world and that was Adam and Jesus, why just those two you ask? You see, Adam started this, and Jesus was the only one who could finish it. When Jesus died on the cross of Calvary, He made a statement, "IT IS FINISHED!!!"

You ask, "What does that mean?" It means that everything that was done to us in the past was now forgiven in the future because of what Jesus has done.

12) Wherefore as by one man sin entered into the world, and death by sin; and so death passed upon all men, for that all have sinned.

13) (For until the law sin was in the world: but sin is not imputed when there is no law.

14) Nevertheless death reigned from Adam to Moses, even after the similitude of Adam's transgression, who is the figure of him that was to come.

15) But not as the offence, so also is the free gift. For if through the offences of one many be dead, much more the grace of God, and the gift by grace, which is by one man, Jesus Christ, hath abounded unto many.

16) And not as it was by one that sinned, so is the free gift: for the judgement was by one to condemnation, but the free gift is of many offences unto justification.

17) For if by one man's offence death reigned by one; much more they which receive abundance

of grace and the gift of righteousness shall reign in life by one, Jesus Christ.)

18) Therefore as by the offence of one judgement came upon all men to condemnation; even so by the righteousness of one the free gift came upon all men unto justification of life.

19) For as by one man's disobedience many were made sinners, so by the obedience of one shall many be made righteous.

Romans 5:14-19. (KJV)

In the book of Romans, it speaks of being saved.

8) But what does it say? The Word (God's message in Christ) is near you, on your lips and in your heart; that is the Word (the message, the basis and object) of faith which we preach,

9) If you acknowledge *and* confess with your lips that Jesus is Lord, and in your heart believe (adhere to, trust in, and rely on the truth) that God raised Him from the dead, you will be saved.

10) For with the heart a person believes (adheres to, trust in, and relies on Christ) and so is justified (declared righteous, acceptable to God), and with the mouth he confesses (declares openly and speaks out freely his faith) *and* confirms [his] salvation.
Romans 10:8-10. (AMPC)

This is the only thing that God asks us to do to receive the finished work which Jesus has done. The only thing that would be your fault is if you don't take advantage of the opportunity that God has given to you to be free of the guilt of sin through Jesus Christ. It's so easy to do. Just confess these words: "I know I am a sinner, and I do believe in you and your son Jesus who died for my sins and that you raised him from the dead. Jesus, come into my heart and give me that life that you died for. I receive it in Jesus' Name, Amen." Now don't worry about trying to do something to please God because you just did.

Philippians 1:6 (NKJV) says, "Being confident of this very thing, that He who has begun a good work in you will complete *it* until the day of Jesus Christ."

Chapter 8:

The Mind

Chapter 8:
The Mind

Study (Colossians 2:4-10).

The preconceived idea of the mind hinders us from knowing that it's about the Spirit of God, which is not mental, but the Spirit of God which is spiritual. This is why faith has to be the foundation of your entire being. How many remember when you began your life in Christ? There wasn't anything you couldn't do. You promised with all your heart to live for Jesus and to tear Satan's kingdom down. At that time in your life, nothing could stop you. Then you were awakened to the realities of human life and the five senses began to really go into play in your life. This is where the real battle happens, in your mind.

6) Now the mind of the flesh [which is sense and reason without the Holy Spirit] is death [death that comprises all miseries arising from sin, both here and hereafter]. But the mind of the Holy Spirit is life and [soul] peace [both now and forever].

7) [That is] because the mind of the flesh [with its carnal thoughts and purposes] is hostile to God, for it does not submit itself to God's Law; indeed it cannot.

8) So then those who are living the life of the flesh [catering to the appetites and impulses of their carnal nature] cannot please *or* satisfy God *or* be acceptable to Him.
Romans 8:6-8 (AMPC)

The mind is the soulish realm of man. This is where your sight, hearing, along with your taste, feelings and smells are controlled. This is the will, intellect, and emotions of man's center point. Enmity is the state or feeling of being opposed or hostile to someone or something.

The mind is a hostile agent to the Spirit of God. Our faith has to be in a power that has no defeat. Now, Faith, is the substance of things hoped for the evidence of things not seen. As we grow in the Lord, we will find out that we first believe which is for salvation. Next, we have faith for the substance. Now we know in whom we believe. Knowing this, or I am persuaded that... (Romans 8:38).

Let's think of the origin of sin. How did it start? It started with the mind being fooled or lied to. Satan spoke to Eve to convince her that she would be as God, knowing good from evil. Eve not knowing that she was already like God because Adam got his start from God, and she came from Adam. Adam came from the breath of God, so both Adam and Eve were created in His likeness. But the only way Satan can talk to you is through your mind. Your spirit, (which is the real you) is signed, sealed, and delivered. You are not a hotel where Jesus checks in and checks out once you do something wrong. This is the reason the Word of God says, you have an advocate with the Father.

1)My Little children, I write you these things so that you may not violate God's law and sin. But if anyone should sin, we have an Advocate (One who will intercede for us) with the Father- [it is] Jesus Christ [the all] righteous [upright, just, Who conforms to the Father's will in every purpose, thought, and action].

2) And He [that same Jesus Himself] is the propitiation (the atoning sacrifice) for our sins, and not for our alone but also for [the sins of] the whole world.
1 John 2:1-2 (AMPC)

Do you remember when Jesus was led into the wilderness by the Holy Ghost to be tempted by the devil? He was bombarded by Satan in His mind. If Jesus was tempted or tried in His mind by Satan, what makes you think that he won't try you? But you have to know who you are, in who you believe, and who and what is on the inside of you. Satan already knows who you are, in whom you believe, and who and what is on the inside of you. He just doesn't want you to know these things. Once you get to know these things, he has no hold on you in your life.

It's time for God's people to inform the devil that he has been unemployed, and that Jesus gave him his pink slip over 2000 years ago.

8) See to it that no one carries you off as spoil *or* makes you yourselves captive by his so-called philosophy *and* intellectualism and vain deceit (idle fancies and plain nonsense), following human tradition (men's ideas of the material rather than the spiritual world), just crude notions following the rudimentary *and* elemental teachings of the universe and disregarding [the teachings of] Christ (the Messiah).

9)For in Him the whole fullness of deity (the Godhead) continues to dwell in bodily form [giving complete expression of the divine nature].

10)And you are in Him, made full *and* having come to fullness of life [in Christ you too are filled with the Godhead-Father, Son and Holy Spirit-and reach full spiritual stature]. And He is the head of all rule and authority [of every angelic principality and power].
Colossians 2:8-10 (AMPC)

God's Love has No Gender

God doesn't love you because of what you do, He loves you because of what He has done. His (God) whole make-up is Love. 1 John 4:7-16. Let's get something straight, while we were yet alienated from the presence of God because of sin, God loved you. But God shows and clearly proves His [own] love for us by the fact that while we were still sinners, Christ (the Messiah, the Anointed One) died for us. Romans 5:8. (AMPC). There was nothing that you did to attain His love, matter of fact, you weren't even born into this world so there was nothing you could have done to bestow God's love on you. God's love has baffled the minds of many and has caused many to think that the only way to get God's love is to work for it. What is there that we could have done to make sure that God's love was guaranteed to be established in our lives? There is nothing at all. What Jesus did on the Cross of Calvary was His guaranteed and eternal love to us.

"For God so loved the world, that he gave his only begotten Son, that whosoever believeth in him should not perish, but have everlasting life. For God sent not his Son into the world to condemn the world, but that the world through him might be saved." John 3:16-17 (KJV)

Let me share something with you.

I was in the kitchen making space in the refrigerator for the pizza that was leftovers of what my granddaughter and I had that night.

The refrigerator was packed to capacity with a little bit of everything. There was coffee from days before and fruit that was going bad and food from dinner that week, like I said the refrigerator was packed. That's not counting the food that we bought that day. I just couldn't find any space in the refrigerator. The only thing I could do to make room for the pizza was to take out the leftovers and other foods that were cluttering up the refrigerator hindering the space for new foods to be placed. I still tried to place the pizza in there without taking out the old and spoiled foods. Regardless of how much I moved things around, there still was not enough space to place the pizza. So, I had to do what I didn't want to do and that was get rid of the old and spoiled foods.

As I started to get rid of the foods that were spoiled and had gone bad, I realized that I didn't need that food anymore. I wasn't going to eat it, it wasn't going to do me any good so why should I keep it? The refrigerator isn't small so there was a lot of food in there that was taking up space. So, I tried to keep the things that I thought were good but when I smelled it, I found that they were bad.

The food had cluttered the refrigerator so much that the refrigerator wasn't work to its full strength to keep the food cold. But when I began to clean the shelving, it started to become colder and back to the temperature it was supposed to be. This that you have read, let it begin to move out some of the clutter of spoiled and rotten thoughts which have blocked your spiritual thinking and are hindering you from becoming who and what you were made to be.

23) And be constantly renewed in the spirit of your mind [having a fresh mental and spiritual attitude],

24) And put on the new nature (the regenerated self) created in God's image, [Godlike] in true righteousness and holiness.

Ephesians 4:23-24 (AMCP)

You will never be able to put fresh information into your mental and spiritual mind until you empty out that which is no longer any help to you.

2) Do not be conformed to this world (this age), [fashioned after and adapted to its external, superficial customs], but be transformed (changed) by the [entire] renewal of your mind [by its new ideals and new attitudes], so that you may prove [for yourselves] what is the good and acceptable and perfect will of God, *even* the thing which is good and acceptable and perfect [in His sight for you]. Romans 12:2 (AMPC)

8) Jesus Christ (the Messiah) is [always] the same, yesterday, today, [yes] and forever (to the ages). Hebrews 13:8 (AMPC)

He never changes, but we do.

For example, the Science Project of NASA have been discovering planets and other solar systems for many years. This is recorded in history of the findings. The only thing wrong with this is observation is NASA has not discovered new planets and solar systems, they are just finding that which was and has been there right after God said, "Let there be light." They are just catching up to where the solar systems and planets have always been, they are just finding out about it.

Finally, the point I am trying to get across to you is the Word of God says, the thing that has been-it is what will be again, and that which has been done is that which will be done again; and there is nothing new under the sun. (Ecclesiastes 1:9 AMPC)

This is what happens when you allow religion to distort your spiritual view of who God really is, which also dims the view of who you really are in Him.

We pray that this reading has challenged you to hear what the Spirit is saying to you and not religion. That you find freedom to be who God created you to be, not in the bondage of religion but in the liberty of living a life of abundance which is God's will for your life!

YOU SHALL **KNOW THE TRUTH** AND THE **TRUTH SHALL MAKE YOU FREE**. John 8:32

Made in the USA
Middletown, DE
09 November 2024

63931272R00046